SPORTS INJURIES:
HOW TO PREVENT, DIAGNOSE, & TREAT

SOCCER

Sports Injuries:
How to Prevent, Diagnose, & Treat

- Baseball
- Basketball
- Cheerleading
- Equestrian
- Extreme Sports
- Field
- Field Hockey
- Football
- Gymnastics
- Hockey
- Ice Skating
- Lacrosse
- Soccer
- Track
- Volleyball
- Weight Training
- Wrestling

SPORTS INJURIES: HOW TO PREVENT, DIAGNOSE, & TREAT

SOCCER

PETE FARROW

MASON CREST PUBLISHERS
www.masoncrest.com

Mason Crest Publishers Inc.
370 Reed Road
Broomall, PA 19008
(866) MCP-BOOK (toll free)
www.masoncrest.com

2 3 4 5 6 7 8 9 10

Farrow, Pete.
Soccer / author, Pete Farrow.
p. cm. — (Sports Injuries)
Summary: Introduces the sport of soccer and provides information on how
to prevent and treat the most common soccer injuries.
Includes bibliographical references and index.

ISBN 1-59084-637-0 (Hardcover : alk. paper)
1. Soccer—Juvenile literature. 2. Soccer injuries—Juvenile
literature. [1. Soccer. 2. Sports injuries.] I. Title. II. Series.
GV943.25.F37 2004
796.344—dc22
2003014578

Project Editor: Michael Spilling
Design: Graham Curd
Picture Research: Natasha Jones

Printed and bound in the Hashemite Kingdom of Jordan

PICTURE CREDITS
Corbis: 6, 8, 13, 14, 16, 18, 21, 22, 24, 25, 26, 29, 31, 32, 33,
36, 38, 40, 41, 42, 49, 51, 52, 54, 56, 57, 59; ©**EMPICS**: 12;
Mary Evans Picture Library: 10; **Topham Picturepoint**: 15.

FRONT COVER: Corbis (bl, br); ©EMPICS (tl); POPPERFOTO (tr).

ILLUSTRATIONS: Courtesy of Amber Books except:
Bright Star Publishing plc: 44, 46, 47, 50.

CONTENTS

Foreword   6

History   8

Preparation to Avoid Injury   18

Getting Ready to Play   30

Equipment   36

Common Injuries and Treatment   42

Your Future in Soccer   54

Glossary   60

Further Information   62

Index   64

Foreword

Sports Injuries: How to Prevent, Diagnose, and Treat is a seventeen-volume series written for young people who are interested in learning about various sports and how to participate in them safely. Each volume examines the history of the sport and the rules of play; it also acts as a guide for prevention and treatment of injuries, and includes instruction on stretching, warming up, and strength training, all of which can help players avoid the most common musculoskeletal injuries. *Sports Injuries* offers ways for readers to improve their performance and gain more enjoyment from playing sports, and young athletes will find these volumes informative and helpful in their pursuit of excellence.

Sports medicine professionals assigned to a sport that they are not familiar with can also benefit from this series. For example, a football athletic trainer may need to provide medical care for a local gymnastics meet. Although the emergency medical principles and action plan would remain the same, the athletic trainer could provide better care for the gymnasts after reading a simple overview of the principles of gymnastics in *Sports Injuries*.

Although these books offer an overview, they are not intended to be comprehensive in the recognition and management of sports injuries. The text helps the reader appreciate and gain awareness of the common injuries possible during participation in sports. Reference material and directed readings are provided for those who want to delve further into the subject.

Written in a direct and easily accessible style, *Sports Injuries* is an enjoyable series that will help young people learn about sports and sports medicine.

Susan Saliba, Ph.D., National Athletic Trainers' Association Education Council

The Brazilian striker Ronaldo holds up the soccer World Cup trophy after his team beat Germany in the 2002 final.

History

Worldwide, soccer is watched by an audience of billions. Indeed, some spend thousands of dollars each year following their team, while others earn millions from playing the game. So where did the sport that Pelé once called "the beautiful game" begin?

Five thousand years ago, the Chinese were kicking around a leather ball filled with hemp. In ancient Greece, an inflated ox bladder was used, while the Egyptians preferred a straw ball and the Aztecs a solid rubber one. It was an American—Charles Goodyear from Connecticut—who produced the first real soccer ball: an inflated rubber sphere covered in leather.

The modern game has its origins in the private schools and universities of England. In 1863, representatives of the country's leading teams met in a London tavern and agreed to play by rules that had been drawn up at Cambridge University seventeen years earlier. And so the first Football Association was born. In those days, goals were narrower and taller, the crossbar was a piece of tape, and the referee was merely a timekeeper who stood on the sidelines. The laws of the game were refined throughout the rest of the century, and they remain subject to review to this day.

In 1871, the first international match took place when Scotland traveled south to face England. In the late 1800s, Britain was the world's major trading nation,

Argentinian midfielder Diego Maradona stands to attention as the Argentine national anthem is played before a game against Mexico in the 1986 World Cup. Argentina went on to win the tournament that year.

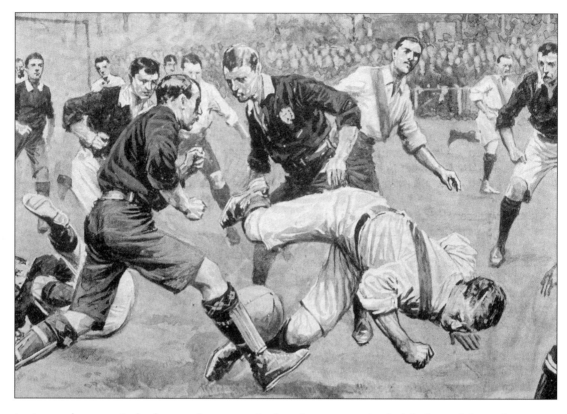

In nineteenth-century England, it was the private schools and universities that laid the basis of the modern game of soccer. Through the influence of the British Empire, it soon became a popular game throughout the world.

and its soldiers, sailors, merchants, and engineers spread soccer across the globe. Athletic Bilbao in Spain, Athletic Club Milan of Italy, and Argentina's River Plate are just a few of the many foreign clubs that have English names. In 1885, the United States played Canada in its first international soccer match and lost 1–0.

The international game is now governed by the *Fédération Internationale de Football Association* (**FIFA**). This was founded in Paris in 1904 by representatives of Belgium, France, Denmark, Holland, Spain, Switzerland, and Sweden. The British nations initially refused to join, and the U.S. Soccer Federation was not formed until 1913.

THE RULES

It is hardly surprising that soccer is loved the world over: it is easy to play and a joy to watch. The poet T.S. Eliot once described soccer as "a science yet beautiful in its art," while the great player Pelé called it "the beautiful game." What makes it beautiful is its simplicity: all it needs are a field of some sort, a ball, and some willing players.

The object of soccer is to score more goals than the opposing team. The goal measures 8 yards (7.3 m) wide and 8 feet (2.4 m) high. A team must defend its own goal and hit the ball into its opponent's. The only player who can handle the ball on the field of play is the goalkeeper, and the goalkeeper is allowed to do this only when the ball is in the penalty box—an 18-yard (16.4-m) area surrounding the goal. A goalkeeper may retain possession of the ball for no more than six seconds at any one time.

Foul play is strictly forbidden. A foul is any illegal action, including striking an opponent; physical contact off-the-ball; handling the ball; dangerous play; and "ungentlemanly conduct," which includes cheating and cursing. Foul play results in a free kick for the opposition, and, if it takes place in the penalty box, it could result in a penalty—a free shot at goal with only the goalkeeper to beat.

If the ball goes out of play, possession passes to the opposing team in the form of a throw-in from the sidelines, or a goal kick or corner. A match lasts for ninety minutes with one fifteen-minute break, although time is added on for any time lost to treating injured players.

Members of the U.S. women's soccer team celebrate winning gold medals in the 1996 Olympic Games after defeating China in the final.

Every Olympic Games since 1900 has featured soccer, except for the 1932 event in Los Angeles. Women's soccer first made an appearance at the Atlanta Games of 1996. Currently, men have to be under the age of twenty-three, and women must be over sixteen, in order to play soccer at the Olympics.

The World Cup is the biggest event in soccer and is held every four years. The first tournament was held in Uruguay in 1930. The country was chosen as host because it had won soccer gold at the Olympic Games of 1924 and 1928. It could not truly be called a "World" Cup because only four teams came from Europe and none from Africa, Asia, or Australasia. The United States did exceptionally well, beating Belgium 3–0 and Paraguay 3–0, before losing 6–1 to Argentina in the semifinal. The Brazilians, however, are the acknowledged masters of the game, having won the World Cup on no fewer than five occasions and produced many of soccer's finest players.

Today, soccer is truly a world game. The 2002 World Cup featured teams from the Americas, Europe, Africa, and Asia, and the television audience numbered in the billions—proving that as a spectator sport, at least, soccer is the most popular game in the world.

THE GREAT PLAYERS

Perhaps the greatest player of all time is Pelé. Born Edson Arantes do Nascimento in Minas Gearais, Brazil in 1940, Pelé became world-famous at the age of seventeen. Starring in the 1958 World Cup, he scored twice in the final, enabling Brazil to win the trophy for the first time. He was also instrumental in ensuring that Brazil won in 1962 and again in 1970. During his 21-year career, he scored 96 goals in 111 international matches and 1,126 goals in all the games he played—a world record that still stands. Pelé had a deep love for the game, and he devoted his life to becoming

Pelé: prime mover behind three of Brazil's World Cup victories and arguably the greatest soccer player of all time.

the best soccer player of all time. This meant practice, dedication to fitness, and focus.

Matthews and Best

The English player Stanley Matthews is unusual in that he played top-level soccer until the age of fifty. He made his debut in the English league in 1938 and retired in 1965, when he was knighted by Queen Elizabeth II for his services to the game. Matthews' subtle body swerves, acceleration, and superb ball control enabled him to beat virtually every player he faced. At the age of forty-one, Matthews won the

Wizard of the dribble, Sir Stanley Matthews was still outwitting defenders at the age of fifty.

first-ever European Player of the Year award. A perfect sportsman, he was never given a **caution** by a referee during his career.

As Sir Stanley's career was drawing to a close, another player fired the imagination of the English public: a skinny kid from Ireland called George Best. With sublime skill, seemingly perfect balance, fearlessness, and incredible self-confidence, Best was the consummate player. When Manchester United won the European Cup in 1968—the greatest prize for a European team—Best was named European Footballer of the Year, at the age of twenty-three. Five years later, Best, a man who could have ruled the soccer world for years to come, gave up world-class soccer and turned his attentions to drinking and other pleasures.

DOUBLE DUTCH

Toward the end of the 1980s, the Dutch were champions, thanks to Marco Van Basten and Ruud Gullit. Twice named World Footballer of the Year, Van Basten won the European title on three occasions. In the 1988 European Championship Final, he scored one of the greatest goals ever seen: the ball floated across the goal from the left, and, from an acute angle, Van Basten volleyed it into the opposite top corner.

However, his career was ended by a severe ankle injury that was not treated properly when it first occurred. He spent much of the 1990s in and out of the hospital, and retired from soccer before the age of thirty.

Gullit captained the Dutch team to European Championship success and was also part of the Milan team that dominated Europe. He enjoyed success in Holland, Italy, and England, despite having troublesome knees. Six times he underwent surgery, but each time he returned—a testament to rapid action, medical science, and, mostly, his dedication and will to play.

Dutch master Marco Van Basten had the world at his feet; however, poor treatment of an ankle injury ruined his career.

Brazilian genius Ronaldo attempts to evade tackles from two Italian defenders as he runs with the ball in a World Cup match in 1998. Brazil went on to lose 3-0 in the final to the host nation, France.

The great Pelé described Best as "the best player in the world," while a leading commentator said, "The only tragedy George Best has to confront is that he will never know how good he could have been."

Diego Maradona

In the 1980s, an Argentinian was the world's greatest player. Indeed, some argue that Diego Armando Maradona was better even than Pelé. Almost single-handedly, he led his country to victory in the 1986 World Cup and turned a struggling Italian club, Napoli, into the champions of Italy. Strong as a bull and fearless, he possessed sublime talent. His world came crashing down when he tested positive for cocaine in 1991. He was suspended from world soccer for fifteen months. He returned to World Cup as Argentine captain in 1994, but was kicked out of the tournament after two games when a drug test found five banned substances. Maradona is still being treated for a cocaine addiction.

The Brazilians

Today, Brazil once again rules the soccer world. Unquestionably, the country's greatest talent is Ronaldo. His breathtaking skill made him a sensation in his own country before he joined teams in Holland and Spain, where he scored goals freely. Named World Player of the Year in both 1996 and 1997, he is the youngest player ever to win the award and the only player to win it in consecutive years. Sensationally, he collapsed on the day of the 1998 World Cup Final and played no part in the match. Ronaldo came back to play club football for Internazionale of Italy, but suffered two serious knee injuries. By 2002, he was back on the world stage and a key player as Brazil won the World Cup for the fifth time. He was named World Player of the Year for a record-breaking third time.

Preparation to Avoid Injury

Soccer can be played by almost anyone. You do not need to be exceptionally tall or muscular, and speed of thought is more important than physical speed. Excellence in performance is a combination of skill and fitness—mental as much as physical.

Kevin Keegan, who was twice named European Player of the Year, is a short man, only 5 ft. 7 in. (1.68 m.). As a young man, he was rejected by several clubs before being drafted by a team in the lower leagues. Eventually, he went on to play for England some sixty-three times. Johann Cruyff was a skinny kid from Amsterdam, Holland, who longed to play for his home-town team, Ajax. He worked at the club for free and asked them if he could play. They refused, arguing that his body was too weak. He worked harder and again he asked—and again. When finally given his chance, he never looked back. Cruyff more than repaid Ajax, helping them to win the European Cup three times and going on to star in the 1974 World Cup.

Some of the game's greats have been short and stocky, including Hungarian wizard Ferenc Puskas and the infamous Diego Maradona. Garrincha—or "songbird," the nickname of Manuel Francisco dos Santos, a Brazilian hero of the

Here, U.S. captain Claudio Reyna controls a high ball in a game in 2001. He was preparing to play a starring role for his team at the 2002 World Cup, but ruptured a cruciate knee ligament, which kept him from participating.

1960s—had bowlegs as a result of polio, but was a sensational player. One of the best players to have graced the English Premiership, Gianfranco Zola, is 5 feet 6 inches (1.66 m) tall and is still going strong at the age of thirty-six, while at 5 feet 2 inches (1.58 m), Tiffeny Milbrett is a top scorer for the U.S. Women's team.

Attitude and ability are the two most important characteristics of any football player. You can be the most talented individual to kick a ball, but your skill will go to waste if you do not apply yourself. Soccer is a team sport, so well-organized teams of average ability can often beat teams of talented individuals that lack unity. In the 2002 World Cup, there were some surprising results. The low-ranked African team, Senegal, beat the reigning World Champion, France; the European giant, Portugal, was beaten by the United States; and hosts South Korea beat the illustrious Italians.

THE FOUR "C"S

How well you succeed in soccer comes down to the four "C"s: commitment, confidence, control, and concentration.

Commitment

1. Have a goal. Visualize what you want to achieve—for example, to be able to shoot a ball where you want to.
2. Start gradually—for example, try shooting at a target over a short distance, and keep practicing until you have mastered it.
3. Increase—in other words, try it from farther distances and different angles.
4. Continue to practice. Even the best players work on their skills regularly, which is what keeps them at the top of their sport.
5. Do not skip training.

Confidence

A key to performing well is the belief that you can do so, and practice will give you this. Indeed, the better control you have over a ball, the more confident you will be.

The commitment, confidence, and concentration of U.S. goalkeeper Brad Friedel cannot be questioned.

When playing another, and perhaps a better, team, remember:

- A team is always only as good as its next game.

- Any opposing team has exactly the same number of players as does your team. And, like you, those players are only human.

- If you play your best, as a team, you can beat the opposition.

- During a soccer game, anything can happen, and it usually does!

- Never lose your will to win: your confidence will gradually drain the belief of your opponents.

It is also worth remembering that attitude can be just as important as skill. So, turn negative thoughts into positives: "I can't do it" becomes "I can do it;" "It's too hot/too muddy" becomes "I can play as well as anyone in these conditions;" "These guys are too good" becomes "It's a tough challenge but we can win;" and finally, as the game draws to a close, "I'm too tired" becomes "I can make one more run."

HEADING THE BALL

When attempting to head the ball, watch it at all times and attempt to judge where it is going.

- standard headers—lean your head back, then bring it forward to meet the ball with your forehead. The power of your header depends on how fast you move your head forward.
- back headers—meet the ball with the rear of the top of your head. Power depends on how quickly you move your head toward the ball.
- side headers—start with your head somewhere near your shoulder, then bring it up to meet the ball when it is upright.
- glancing headers—your head should meet the ball and attempt to steer it in another direction. A lack of height is not a disadvantage if you have the right timing, the ability to hang in the air, and sufficient power. England's Michael Owen, for example, is not particularly tall, but he heads the ball well.

John Carew (left), of Valencia and Norway, demonstrates a classic glancing header as he out-jumps Lauren (Arsenal and Cameroon).

Control

To become familiar with the ball takes practice—on your own and with others. Soccer is a team game, but you can learn many of the skills by yourself. Remember, when you train by yourself, no one is criticizing you. You can motivate yourself, and experiment while you learn.

First, get used to the feel of the ball by rolling it around using the sole of your foot and your instep. This will also help to develop ankle flexibility. Now try kicking it against a wall. The ball will rebound, teaching you how to control and strike the ball. Play "one-twos" with yourself by kicking the ball at the wall at an angle and collecting the "return pass."

When kicking a ball, there are two important points to note:

- For power, kick with the instep of the foot. Never kick with the toe—this hurts, and there is no telling where the ball will end up.

- For greater accuracy, use the inside of the foot. You can also use the outside of the foot and, occasionally, to surprise your opponents, your heel, kicking the ball behind you.

Learn to control the ball by yourself—**juggling** is one way of doing so. Alternate between small and high bounces, and use your thigh and foot to juggle the ball.

Now you need to learn how to move with the ball. First, try **dribbling**. Put down a few objects, and try dribbling through them, using one foot or both feet. This exercise will help you to establish a rhythm. Now practice different ways of turning with a ball under your control.

Try a sequence—juggling, turning, controlling the ball—and use a small ball, perhaps a tennis ball, to sharpen your control. Improve your body movement by using a ball that is not moving. For example, put the ball on the ground and come

You can pick up a lot of ideas for technique and tricks by watching the top players in action. Here, a striker attempts to score a goal by powering the ball with the outside of his foot.

up to it, then pass one leg around and over the ball and move away. The ball should remain still.

Finally, learn from the top players. You can pick up some of soccer's more spectacular tricks, such as flicking the ball up in the air. Watch how the top players do these tricks, and then try them yourself.

Now comes the time to practice with others. For **shooting**, **passing**, heading, and **tackling**, you will need at least one more player. Try passing to each other at different angles, heights, and distances. See how long you can keep the ball up in the air between you, using only your heads, chests, and feet. Throw the ball to

TACKLING

Tackling means blocking another player who has the ball, then trying to come away with it. You must touch the ball before the player, otherwise it is a foul. Using the bottom of your foot to tackle is also a foul because it could result in serious injury.

- block tackles—using your foot to rob a player of the ball, by blocking the progress of the ball.
- 50/50 ball—when the ball is equidistant from you and your opponent, you obviously want to get there first. If you can, try to make a short pass to one of your teammates; if not, go for a block tackle.
- interceptions—taking control of the ball when it is passed or dribbled.
- barging—it is legal to lean into a player with your shoulder when he has the ball. Hitting, however, is not allowed, but you can couple leaning with a sliding tackle.

Tackling from behind is illegal and will result in a free kick for the opposition and probably a caution for you.

A sliding tackle can look spectacular, but must be timed to perfection. Practice your tackling, particularly your timing.

Agility is a key quality of soccer players—especially goalkeepers, who might be called upon to make a match-saving stop at any time in the game.

each other to practice headers. And if there are only a few of you, play with smaller goals—this sharpens skills. Always remember that soccer is a team sport. The more your timing improves, the less likely you are to sustain injury.

Concentration

You need not be exceptionally quick or strong to play soccer. The best players are able to anticipate what is going to happen, and so are able to move into position for the ball before anyone else. So pay attention, and do not let your mind wander: the more aware you are, the more you can make good passes. Know where your teammates are, and you will be able to make a simple but killer pass.

In short:

- Know your position and stick to the shape of the team.
- When your team has the ball, make runs into space so that you can receive a pass.
- Always support your teammates: soccer is a team game.
- When the opposition has the ball, get into positions that win it back.
- When you are tired, you lose concentration: be in the best shape to play the game and stay focused.

KEEPING FIT

To play at any reasonable level of soccer requires fitness. Getting fit involves turning your limitations into your strengths. Fit players have the fewest injuries. Soccer is unusual in that it requires both stamina—the ability to run for long periods of time—and explosive speed—running quickly over short distances.

A lack of fitness means that you will tire more quickly. When bodies are tired, they are more likely to be injured. Sudden changes in speed and direction put players at risk of joint or muscle injury.

The best players are able to stay on their feet; this really helps during a game. Physiologists call the best point of balance "core stability." You can find yours by imagining that a balloon filled with helium is pulling your head upward. Core stability is the basis of body control.

Increasing stamina does not take much "moderate intensity activity" (**M.I.A.**). M.I.A. makes you feel warm and breathe more heavily than usual. More vigorous activity is fine, as long as you feel okay and are still able to talk—this is known as your comfort zone. If you are unable to do this, you are probably working at too high an intensity. Ideally, you should be aiming for one hour of moderate intensity activity each day. You do not have to do one hour of activity all at one time. For example, you could build up to one hour by ten minutes of walking to school; twenty minutes of sports at lunchtime; ten minutes walking home from school; and twenty minutes of dancing to your favorite music, or cycling.

Every little bit helps, but do try to include some activity that is nonstop for ten to fifteen minutes. This will exercise your heart, boosting your stamina so that your body is able to function more effectively with less risk of injury.

Explosive speed

On the soccer field, you will also need explosive speed. Practice short sprints. Be sure that you warm up first and aim to run as fast as you can over 5–10 yards (4.5–9 m). Stop, then rest for ten seconds and run again. Once you have mastered this exercise, try sprinting over the same distance, then turning 180° to run back to the start. This will help to build your energy levels and your ability to recover from this kind of activity.

Soccer involves many rapid changes of direction, so it is vital that your body is flexible. Flexibility is the ability to move your joints freely and without pain,

Women from leading American college team the SMU Mustangs stretch their muscles before playing. Flexible muscles are less likely to sustain an injury.

stiffness, or resistance. Flexible muscles are less prone to soreness and injury because they are actually longer and less likely to tear or strain than short, inflexible muscles. Think of muscles as an elastic band. A too-tight band is likely to snap or break when you stretch it, unless you gradually stretch and release it to make it more supple.

Avoid joint problems by exercising your joints and keeping your muscles strong. Swimming is a good way of loosening joints, while gentle running is especially good at keeping your knees and ankles flexible. Cycling is also helpful. Remember, you must seek assistance if you have any inflammation of your joints or feel any pain in your muscles after exercise.

Getting Ready to Play

Soccer is an athletic game and athletes need the correct fuel to function properly. If you put the wrong type of gas into a car, the car will not work as it should. Likewise, the wrong kind of diet will affect your performance.

Staying in shape means eating and drinking the right things and avoiding those things that are bad for you. A healthy, balanced diet does not mean giving up all of your favorites—it is the balance that counts.

Eating provides you with energy, which is quickly burned off by exercise. If the food you eat provides more energy than you use up, then you will put on weight. Your body always uses glucose for energy. The best way to keep your stores of glucose stocked up is to eat a diet rich in carbohydrates and low in fats.

When exercising, 75 percent of energy is lost as heat. When you get hot and sweat, on average you lose 2 pints (1 l) of fluid for each hour you exercise, which represents a loss of 2 pounds 3 ounces (1 kg) of body weight. For a person who weighs 154 pounds (70 kg), a loss of just two percent in body weight—3 pounds (1.4 kg) or 3 pints (1.4 l)—will affect the ability to exercise. For every one percent drop in body weight, you will suffer a five percent drop in performance!

If you are playing, ensure that you regularly replenish your fluid levels, preferably with fruit juice, a sports drink, or water. Sugary sodas will only make

A few minutes of stretching before a game can help you avoid months off the team as a result of injury.

GOOD FUEL, BAD FUEL

Good Fuel:

- lowfat dairy products;
- eggs;
- fish;
- meat and poultry with little or no fat;
- cereals, including corn;
- vegetables, including peas and beans;
- potatoes: boiled or baked;
- rice;
- legumes;
- bread, bagels;
- pasta;
- fruit;
- honey;
- water, milk, fruit juice, or sports drink.

Bad Fuel:

- any foods with lots of fat— including butter and cream;
- burgers, sausages, salami;
- chips and fries;
- sugary candies;
- chocolate;
- soda pops;
- drinks with caffeine, including coffee and cola.

Pasta is an excellent prematch meal because it provides the complex carbohydrates the body needs to sustain energy for a 90-minute match.

The Brazilian team who won the 1994 World Cup prove that top stars stay at the top by training hard.

you thirstier. Remember, in hot temperatures, you lose fluid more quickly. If you do not replace it, you could end up in a hospital with dehydration.

WARMING UP

A half-hour or so before the match, it is crucial that you begin to warm up. Cold muscles are easily torn or snapped. Warming up means exactly that: doing light exercise that will raise your body temperature. Start with brisk walking. Next, break into a gentle trot. Finally, sprint. Then try exercises that loosen up your joints: shoulder rotations, side bends, torso twists, and knee lifts. Below are some stretching exercises that will help you stay injury-free during the game:

Side straddle

Sit with your legs spread. Hold one ankle with both hands and bring your knee toward your chin, keeping the leg straight. Hold for five seconds. Repeat five times. Do the same for your other leg. This helps to loosen your shoulders and stretch your calves and **hamstrings**.

Seat stretch

Sit with your legs together, straight out in front of you. Hold each ankle and bring your chin toward your knees. Hold for five seconds, then repeat five times. This helps to loosen your back muscles.

Quad stretch

Lie on your back with one leg straight, then bend your other leg to 90° and press your knee to floor. Hold for five seconds, then repeat five times. Do the same for your other leg. This helps to loosen your **quadriceps**.

Knees to chest

Lie on your back, then bend your knees and bring them toward your chest. Hold this position for five seconds, then repeat five times. This helps to loosen the muscles in your lower back and stretches your stomach muscles.

Seat stretches can help you to avoid calf and hamstring strains, as well as help to loosen your back muscles before playing.

Forward lunge

With one leg bent to 90°, stretch your other leg back as far as you can, with your foot on the floor. Lean forward and hold for five seconds. Repeat five times. Reverse the position of your legs, and repeat. This will help you to avoid groin strains.

Thigh stretch

Stand with your feet apart, with one leg straight and the other bent to 90°. Hold this position for five seconds, then repeat five times. Reverse the position of your legs and repeat. This will help you to avoid thigh and hamstring strains.

Hamstring and calf stretch

Stand up straight, with your feet crossed, but together. Touch your toes and hold this position for five seconds. Repeat five times. Reverse the position of your feet and repeat. This will help you to avoid hamstring and calf strains.

Calf stretch

Lean against a wall, with your hands straight out in front of you and one leg bent to 90°. Stretch your other leg back as far as you can, keeping your foot on the floor. Hold for five seconds, then repeat five times. Reverse the position of your legs and repeat. This will help you to avoid calf strains.

A good way to give your quads a workout—and avoid groin strains—is with some forward lunges.

Equipment

The correct equipment will not only help you perform well, but will protect you from injury as well. Soccer shoes are the major tools of the soccer player's trade, while equipment such as shin pads will protect the lower legs.

A good soccer shoe will:

- fully cover the foot;
- have a rigid heel;
- be flexible at the front of the foot;
- have a wide sole;
- be well padded at the instep, sides, and heel;
- be made of leather;
- fit snugly because ill-fitting shoes cause injury.

PLAYING SURFACES

Soccer is played on various surfaces, and different types of shoes are needed for each one. Make sure that your shoes are appropriate to the playing surface, giving the best traction possible.

Short grass is the traditional playing surface for soccer because the ball moves over it quickly. If you slip on this surface, though, you could suffer strains, sprains, or muscle tears. The best type of soccer shoe to use is one with molded

Having the correct equipment greatly reduces the risk of injuring yourself or others. Goalkeepers usually wear gloves to protect their hands from powerful shots.

Traction, balance, and control are all enhanced by the correct footwear. The right shoes will also help you to avoid injury.

cleats. Soccer shoes with screw-in cleats can also be used to provide better grip, which is needed for playing on long grass or wet grass.

Astroturf can be slippery when wet and is also a fairly hard surface. If you fall on it, you could suffer friction burns. There are special astroturf soccer shoes designed for this surface. These have either knobbed soles or multicleats.

Hard ground, including dirt or concrete, will put a lot of pressure on your joints, especially your knees and ankles. The most appropriate footwear is soccer shoes with ribbed soles or molded rubber-soled soccer shoes.

Indoor soccer fields made from wood or composite material also put pressure on your joints. Again, molded, rubber-soled soccer shoes with thick soles provide the best protection.

OTHER EQUIPMENT

Shin guards, or shin pads, are another essential piece of equipment. Most players who suffer injuries to their lower legs are not protected by adequate shin guards. Make sure that your guards fit properly. The best type of shin guards includes ankle pads, which offer protection and support to your ankles. Ankle pads can also be bought separately.

Modern soccer socks are made from a fabric that is tight-fitting, enabling it to

LOOKING AFTER YOUR SOCCER SHOES

Soccer shoes are a soccer player's best friend. Make sure that you look after them between games:

- When you take them off, untie the laces properly.
- Remove soil or mud by banging the shoes against a wall, and use a brush to get the rest off. Then wipe the shoes with a damp cloth. Never use soap or detergent to clean your soccer shoes—you will damage the leather.
- If they are wet, stuff them with newspaper (to keep them in shape), and allow them to dry. Do not dry them with a hair dryer, for example—you could crack them.
- When dry, polish and coat them with a waterproof polish or spray.
- If your shoes have screw-in cleats, grease them occasionally to prevent rusting.
- Damaged cleats can cause serious injury—replace broken ones.
- Never overtighten screw-in cleats—you will damage the threads.
- Avoid walking on hard surfaces, such as concrete or stone, when you are wearing cleats, because this will make them dangerously sharp.

hold your pads in place. While this fabric gives a firm grip, it also allows your feet and legs to breathe and allows any moisture to escape. Shorts should be loose-fitting for maximum mobility. If you would like extra support for your thighs and groin area, consider wearing spandex shorts under your soccer shorts. Cycling shorts offer similar support and are popular with some players.

Take good care of your uniform and keep your equipment clean and well-maintained at all times.

Shirts and shorts are light and porous, enabling moisture to escape and the garments to stay dry. They are specifically designed for comfort and performance. Some players choose to wear undershirts, especially in cold weather. These should also be light-weight and allow moisture to escape, thus keeping you dry and cool in hot weather, but dry and warm in cold weather. If you want one, choose an undershirt with little or no seam, to reduce chaffing.

Female soccer players should also wear a suitable sports bra, and consider a supportive sports undershirt.

The ball

Balls come in three different sizes, ranging from size three, the smallest, to size five, which is used in professional games. When learning, select the ball size that is most comfortable for you.

Different balls are appropriate for different playing surfaces. On grass, a leather ball with a waterproof coating is most suitable. On a concrete or other hard outdoor surface, choose a plastic one that is "regulation weight." On wooden surfaces indoors, there are specially made balls that have a covering similar to tennis balls.

GOALKEEPERS

Goalies require specific equipment of their own. Soccer shoes should preferably have screw-in, long cleats because the mouth of the goal can get very muddy. Shin guards should also be worn.

On hard playing fields, long pants are the best option. These provide padding down the sides of the legs, for cushioning dives. On normal playing fields, shorts should be worn. These, too, have padding and provide protection.

A goalkeeper's jersey must be a different color from either of the teams playing. Goalie jerseys should also provide padding, especially down the arms and the sides.

Gloves are one of the essential parts of goalkeeping equipment. They are specifically designed for goalies. The gloves that you choose should have a rubber covering at the front and should also be well padded. Try to ensure that you obtain ones that have a fastening at the wrist.

In very sunny weather, you may want to wear a hat to keep the sun out of your eyes.

Soccer goalkeepers can take a beating during a game—if this is your role, always be sure that you are adequately protected.

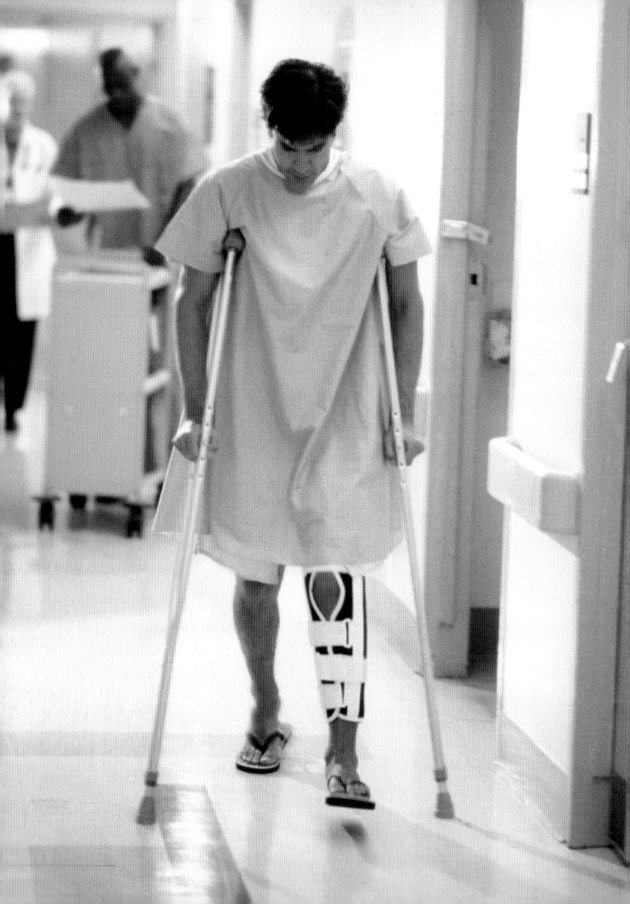

Common Injuries and Treatment

Soccer is a physical contact sport. You will be very fortunate if you avoid having some kind of injury during your playing career. Preparation and discipline will go a long way toward protecting you, and it is estimated that about three-quarters of all soccer injuries could be prevented.

Most injuries are relatively minor, but do not be afraid of seeking professional help. In the United States, about 500,000 soccer injuries require medical treatment each year.

Minor injuries can be easily treated using the **P.R.I.C.E.** method:

P, for Protection—stop training immediately; avoid all unnecessary activity.

R, for Rest—take the weight off the injury.

I, for Ice—apply an ice pack for about twenty minutes; repeat each hour for four hours.

C, for Compression—wrap the injury with a bandage or tape.

E, for Elevation—raise the injured body part in order to reduce swelling.

FOOT

Bruising is the most common foot injury in soccer, and it can be treated by the P.R.I.C.E. method.

Certain severe injuries require hospital treatment, but many injuries can be avoided by taking proper precautions.

ANKLE LIGAMENTS

Strong ankle ligaments are a great aid to balance and control of a soccer ball.

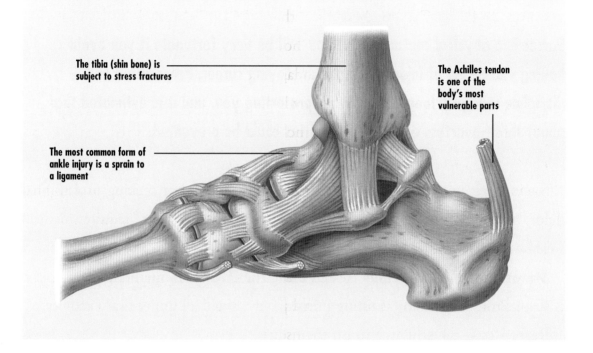

The tibia (shin bone) is subject to stress fractures

The Achilles tendon is one of the body's most vulnerable parts

The most common form of ankle injury is a sprain to a ligament

A sharp burning pain in the sole of the foot is likely to be as a result of a cracked metatarsal—one of the long bones leading to your toes. This kind of break is called a stress fracture. The only treatment in this case is to stay off your foot for a while: use crutches for a week or so. The fracture can take six to twelve weeks to heal completely.

If the base of your heel is very tender, this is a sign of an inflamed tendon. You will need to rest your foot for a week or so, and take **anti-inflammatory** medication. Try rolling your feet back and forth over cans of frozen juice a few times a day, to reduce the pain and swelling.

ANKLE

The most common form of ankle injury is a sprain. A sprain is caused by the stretching and/or tearing of the ankle **ligaments**. This is characterized by joint instability, pain, and swelling.

Follow the P.R.I.C.E. method. Take the weight off the ankle; if necessary, do not let it bear weight for twenty-four hours or more. Apply ice treatment. Tape up the ankle, preferably with a bandage. Finally, elevate it: this will reduce bleeding and help to reduce swelling by letting fluids flow away.

Medical treatment for sprains includes anti-inflammatory medication, **ultrasound** treatment, massage, and **physical therapy**.

A broken or fractured ankle is characterized by immediate and sudden pain, severe bruising, tenderness to the touch, and great pain if weight is put on it. The leg should be elevated, and a splint should be fitted if available. Expert medical treatment is required. A broken ankle takes about six weeks to heal fully, but it will be several months before you could play soccer again.

The Achilles tendon connects the muscles in the lower leg with the heel bone. Tendons can be strained or ruptured. If your Achilles is strained, it will be tender and may be swollen, and you will have pain when you rise up on your toes. Use the P.R.I.C.E. method to treat it.

If, however, an Achilles is ruptured, you will feel it snap and will be unable to raise your heel or point your toes. The foot should be raised and rested immediately, and expert medical treatment should be obtained. Surgery may be necessary, though this injury can often be treated by putting the leg in a cast for a period of time. A rupture can take up to ten months to heal, and more time would be needed to get back into shape before the injured person could play soccer again.

LOWER LEG

Shinsplints are a type of muscle strain that causes pain at the front of the lower leg. The most common cause is inflammation from overuse or from running on hard surfaces. Shinsplints are characterized by pain, swelling, lumps, and redness over the inside of the shin. Use the P.R.I.C.E. method to reduce pain. Heat treatment should also be used and the shin taped until swelling is reduced. Medical treatment includes anti-inflammatory medication, massage, and physical therapy.

Calf

Calf strains are characterized by a sharp pain. For treatment, use the P.R.I.C.E. method. Keep weight off of the leg for two days, and take anti-inflammatory medication. After the pain and swelling have subsided, you can resume some light exercise, but do not overdo things.

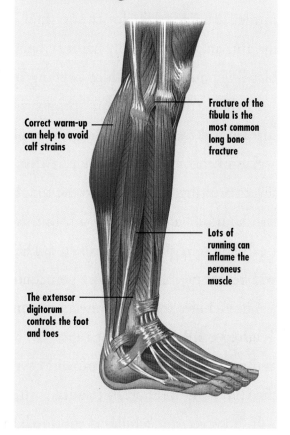

LOWER LEG MUSCLES

The essential power necessary for playing soccer comes from the lower leg.

Correct warm-up can help to avoid calf strains

Fracture of the fibula is the most common long bone fracture

Lots of running can inflame the peroneus muscle

The extensor digitorum controls the foot and toes

Knee

The most common form of knee injury is patellafemoral pain syndrome, or runner's knee. Amongst adolescent soccer players, the second most common injury is Osgood Schlatter Disease, a pain and bump below the knee cap. Use P.R.I.C.E. for minor damage, which will heal in a few days. Severe injury, characterized by sharp pain and much swelling, requires medical treatment. Extreme cases will need surgery. Other treatments include ultrasound and physical therapy.

Ligaments can also be damaged, including the medial collateral ligament, which is on the inside of the knee, and the lateral collateral ligament, which is on the outside. If injured, these will be sore to the touch and painful when the knee is bent. Immediate treatment should be P.R.I.C.E. The leg needs to be rested from sporting activity for three to eight weeks. A serious sprain

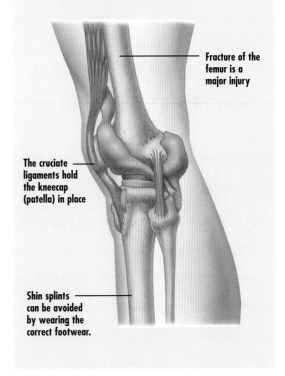

ANATOMY OF THE KNEE

The knees are the body's shock absorbers, and they are easily strained and injured.

Fracture of the femur is a major injury

The cruciate ligaments hold the kneecap (patella) in place

Shin splints can be avoided by wearing the correct footwear.

will require surgery, followed by three months' rest and rehabilitation.

Anterior cruciate ligament injuries are the most severe knee damage. These are caused by twisting or receiving a blow to the knee and are characterized by joint instability, swelling, and severe pain, especially when the lower leg is moved. Treat these injuries immediately with the P.R.I.C.E. method and seek medical help. This kind of injury typically requires surgery, and you may take up to twelve months to be ready to play again.

THIGH

Contusions—also known as dead legs—are a common injury in any contact sport, caused when muscle is crushed against the bone. These vary in severity. Minor ones, characterized by minor pain, can be treated quickly using the P.R.I.C.E. method until pain subsides, and then by doing some quad stretches, as long as these do not cause pain. Serious contusions involve severe pain and swelling, and require immediate medical attention. Treatment includes ultrasound, massage, and, in extreme cases, surgery. Recovery can require days or months, depending on how bad the injury is.

OVERUSE INJURIES

An overuse, or chronic, injury is caused by repeating the same action many times. This is not as serious as an acute injury, but any chronic problem may become worst if not acknowledged early on, so players should seek medical advice and treatment. Overuse injuries have both mental and physical symptoms:

- unusual tiredness or fatigue
- feeling very emotional, particularly depressed, anxious, or stressed
- a lack of appetite
- an inability to sleep at night
- muscle soreness and cramps
- stiff, painful, or unstable joints
- painful tendons
- pain that shows no improvement for more than three days

Injuries can occur at any time and at any level in a soccer game. This defender has injured his knee while tackling another player in an amateur game.

Thigh strains are tears of the quadricep muscles. The symptoms are similar to contusions. For minor injuries, P.R.I.C.E. will produce results, but a return to full fitness will take three to six weeks. A major tear may require surgery and take up to three months to repair. Ultrasound and massage are also used in treatment.

Hamstring strains are characterized by a sharp pain in that area and an inability to move without pain. These too can be minor or very serious. Whatever the nature of the strain, use P.R.I.C.E. The amount of swelling shows how serious the injury is. Severe cases require immediate medical attention. Ultrasound, massage, and physical therapy are used to treat these injuries. Recovery can be a matter of days, or can require up to three months, depending on the severity of the strain.

Anyone recovering from a thigh injury should consider wearing spandex shorts or cycling shorts under their normal soccer shorts. These will help to prevent further thigh injuries.

GROIN

Groin strains are ruptures of the adductor muscles, caused when the muscles are stretched too far. They are similar to thigh strains and their treatment is much the same. A minor one will cause slight pain, but a serious groin strain will leave you unable to walk. P.R.I.C.E. is the best initial treatment. Serious strains require immediate medical help, and may require surgery. Lesser injuries can take three to six weeks to recover; where surgery is needed, the minimum recovery time will be three months.

GROIN STRAIN

Soccer's most common injury, groin strains often cause players to miss months of the season.

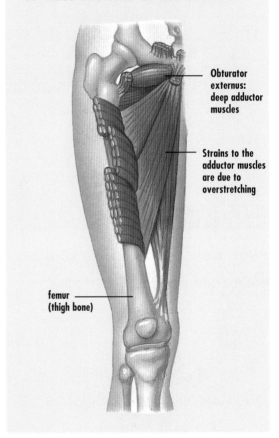

Obturator externus: deep adductor muscles

Strains to the adductor muscles are due to overstretching

femur (thigh bone)

A hernia is when tissue breaks through the wall of stomach muscles. The symptoms are a lump in either the groin area or the stomach. The only treatment for this condition is surgery. Immediate medical attention is required, and surgery is the only treatment. Recovery can take months.

Spandex shorts or cycling shorts can also help in recovery from groin injuries.

TORSO

Abdominal muscle strains are tears in the stomach muscles. They are similar to thigh and calf strains, and are characterized by tightness, pain, and, sometimes, bruising. P.R.I.C.E. is the way to treat these strains. Injuries require about two weeks' rest and, depending on the seriousness, may take up to six weeks for full recovery.

A stress fracture of the lower back is called spondylolisthesis. It is characterized by an ache that is made worse by playing sports. Rest is the great cure—six weeks is often sufficient—but you will also have to strengthen the back muscles. Physical therapy is a good aid to recovery.

The knees bear much of the pressure in a typical soccer game. A knee injury should be immediately treated with the P.R.I.C.E. treatment method, to ensure the damage does not worsen.

Certain clashes of heads can have serious consequences: if you feel at all groggy or disoriented, you should seek medical attention immediately.

Falling onto the shoulder, elbow, or an outstretched arm can sprain the acromio-clavicular joint—a joint in the shoulder. A sprain can range in severity from minor pain to a complete rupture of the joint, in which case you will get a lump near the neck. The P.R.I.C.E. treatment, coupled with some shoulder exercises, can deal with minor sprains. Serious injuries require medical treatment and will involve the shoulder being strapped with a bandage or tape. Serious injuries may also require surgery.

BROKEN BONES

A broken bone is a serious injury that requires immediate medical attention. The best thing to do is protect the injured area. Do not move it: you could make the injury worse. A brace or splint should be fitted, if these are available. If the bone has broken the skin—producing an open fracture—do not wash or probe the injured area. Cover it with a clean cloth and tie a bandage over it to stop the bleeding. Medical treatment will include a plaster cast for about six weeks, and it will take a few months to get in shape again for soccer.

HEAD

Concussion can be caused by blows to the head, face, or neck. There are no outward symptoms, but a player may be unaware of where she is or of what day it is, and experience "fogginess" or dizziness. Players should immediately be removed from play and watched closely. If the situation does not improve, medical attention should be sought.

Broken noses are characterized by bruising and swelling of the skin of the nose. Immediate treatment is to stop the blood flow by plugging the nostrils and applying an ice-pack to stop swelling. If the fracture seems serious, seek medical attention, particularly if the nose is flattened.

Your Future in Soccer

Soccer is the fastest growing sport in the United States. The number of players has quadrupled in the past ten years to more than nineteen million; the only team sport that attracts more players is basketball. Soccer is a multicultural sport, drawing players and fans from all ethnic backgrounds.

The United States has the largest number of soccer coaches in the world, and across the country there are thousands of teams. Every state has its own soccer association. Major League Soccer (MLS) recently celebrated its tenth anniversary and is growing stronger and stronger, attracting an increasing number of supporters and some of the country's top athletes.

In the past decade, the United States has become a force in world soccer. The men's national team has competed in the final stages of the last four World Cups. In 2002, it finished in the top eight—a result that was not matched by many powerful soccer nations, including Argentina, Holland, Italy, and Portugal. The women's team is world-class, having won two of the three women's World Cups and Olympic Gold. The women's youth team won the first-ever FIFA Under-19 Women's World Championship. Leading U.S. women players Tiffeny Milbrett and Mia Hamm are recognized as among the best in the world.

Mia Hamm started playing for the U.S. National Women's team at the age of fifteen and is one of the world's best female players.

The European Leagues, which traditionally attract the world's best players, are increasingly recruiting Americans. In the 1990s, John Harkes enjoyed a successful career in England. U.S. captain Claudio Reyna has graced the leagues of Germany, Scotland, and England. Goalkeeper Brad Friedel has played in Turkey and in England, where he is a top star. Brian McBride is also currently wowing the crowds in England. Most leading soccer players began their careers at, or before, high school.

Soccer can be played anywhere by anyone, but if you are looking for a career in the game it is best to find a local team. Here, you will be able to get some coaching. If you have no luck in finding a team near to you, check out the U.S. Youth Soccer Association's website: www.usysa.org. This has links to all state

Soccer is the fastest growing sport in the United States, as more and more people find themselves falling in love with "the beautiful game."

BRIAN MCBRIDE

Here, the United States' national team poses before a game in 2002. American goal machine Brian McBride (no. 20) broke records as a teenager and he now enjoys a lucrative career playing soccer in Europe.

Born in Arlington Heights, Illinois, in 1972, McBride attended Lee Buffalo Grove High School, where he scored eighty goals. At St. Louis University, he set a record for goal scoring and played for the college's All Conference Side for three years. Since 1993, he has played for the U.S. national team, including the World Cups of 1998 and 2002. A six-time MLS All-Star, he was awarded MLS Goal of the Year in 1998.

Professional career:

1994–1995	VfL Wolfsburg, Germany
1996–present	Columbus Crew
2000–2001	Preston North End, England
2002–present	Everton, England

TIFFENY MILBRETT

Born in Portland, Oregon, in 1972, Tiffeny Milbrett studied at the University of Portland, where she was a three-time NSCAA All-American. She has played in the U.S. national team since 1991, playing in more than one hundred games and scoring 96 goals, including the winning goal in the Olympic Games Final. She was U.S. Soccer's Chevy Female Athlete of the Year for 2000 and 2001, and won the ESPY Award for the Best Female Soccer Player in 2002.

Professional career:

1995–1997   Shiroki Serena, Japan

2001–present   New York Power

organizations for youth soccer. There are also a growing number of summer camps that offer soccer coaching.

THE COLLEGE SCENE

There is a vibrant soccer scene at college, with more than 2,500 colleges playing the game—indeed, there are more soccer than football teams. Among the leading colleges for male soccer are Boston College, Clemson, North Carolina, St. John's, St. Louis, Stanford, U.C.L.A., and Virginia. Leading colleges for women's soccer include the University of Connecticut, Penn State, Pepperdine, Portland, Stanford, Santa Clara, University of Tennessee, Texas A. & M., and U.C.L.A. Around 50,000 soccer scholarships are available at colleges, provided by certain

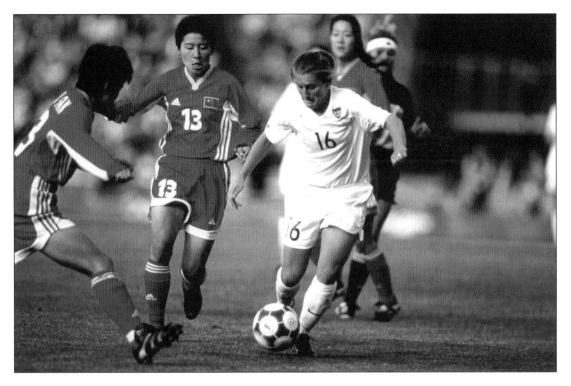

Tiffeny Milbrett attempts to dribble past two defenders as the U.S. women's soccer team plays China during the final match of the 2000 Olympic Games in Australia.

local soccer associations. Scholarships generally cover four years and can amount to $30,000 worth of tuition fees, books, and room and board. These scholarships are awarded on the basis of both academic achievement and athletic ability. The **U.S. Soccer Federation** offers some young people the chance to graduate into the professional game straight from high school. There are also many amateur teams in all states looking for players.

Soccer, above all, is about fun. You can have the best fun if you are fit and injury-free, whether playing in a World Cup Final or just having fun with friends. Take time to develop your skills, work on your fitness, and, above all, prepare well, and you will discover just how beautiful "the beautiful game" actually is.

Glossary

Anti-inflammatory: Any medication that reduces swelling.

Caution: Players receive a penalty (also known as a booking) for serious offences or persistent fouling; the referee gives the warning by showing a yellow card; two penalties result in an immediate dismissal—also known as being "thrown out of the game."

Corner: A free kick awarded to the attacking side if the ball crosses the end line after being touched by the defending side.

Dangerous play: Actions by a player that the referee deems unsafe—for example, high kicking, recklessness.

Dribbling: Running at and past opponents with the ball.

FIFA: *Fédération Internationale de Football Association*, the governing body of world soccer, which decides the rules of the game and organizes the World Cup.

Foul: Any illegal action, including handling the ball and any physical contact with an opponent off-the-ball, as well as kicking, striking, tripping, holding, pulling, pushing, and spitting at opponents, or attempting to do so.

Free kick: A direct free kick is awarded against teams who have fouled or handled the ball; a goal can be scored directly from a free kick; an indirect free kick is given for minor fouls, such as deliberately obstructing another player; the ball must be touched by two different players for a goal to be scored from it.

Goal kick: A kick taken from the six-yard line by one of the defending team if the ball has crossed the six-yard line after being touched by the attacking side; it must go farther than the penalty box.

Hamstrings: The group of three muscles set at the back of the thigh.

Juggling: Keeping the ball up in the air using any part of the body except the arms.

Ligament: A short band of tough body tissue, which connects bones or holds together joints.

M.I.A.: Abbreviation for "moderate intensity activity," which will increase stamina.

Passing: Playing the ball to a teammate using the foot, leg, chest, or head.

Penalty: A free kick at goal from 12 yards (11 m); the goalkeeper must be on his line and every other player, except the kicker, must be 10 yards (9.1 m) behind the penalty mark.

Penalty box: Also known as the 18-yard box, this marks an area of 18 yd. (16.4 m) around the goal; goalkeepers are allowed to handle the ball only in this area.

Physical therapy: The treatment of an injury or illness using physical techniques such as massage and stretching, rather than medicines or surgery.

P.R.I.C.E.: Acronym for an effective way to treat many simple injuries—Protection, Rest, Ice, Compression, and Elevation.

Quadriceps: A large four-part muscle on the front of the thigh, which is used to extend the leg.

Shooting: Attempting to score a goal.

Tackling: Stealing the ball from an opponent.

Ultrasound: Sound waves that are outside the range of human hearing; physical therapists sometimes use ultrasound machines to treat damaged muscles by sending sound waves vibrating through the injured area.

U.S. Soccer Federation: The governing body of soccer in the United States.

Volley (v.): To kick the ball when it is in the air; some spectacular goals are scored this way.

Further Information

USEFUL WEB SITES

A very good Dutch site, written in English: www.bettersoccermorefun.com

Major League Soccer: www.mlsnet.com

The official site of U.S. soccer coaches: www.nscaa.com

For tips and tactics: www.soccerhelp.com

The U.S. Soccer Federation: www.ussoccer.com

The U.S. Youth Soccer Association: www.usysa.org

The Women's United Soccer Association: www.wusa.com

The Web sites listed on this page were active at the time of publication. The publisher is not responsible for Web sites that have changed their address or discontinued operation since the date of publication. The publisher will review and update the Web sites upon each reprint.

FURTHER READING

Ekblom, Bjorn. *Handbook Of Sports Medicine and Science: Soccer.* London: Blackwell Science, 1994.

Fleck, Thomas et al. *Official U.S. Youth Soccer Coaching Manual.* Richardson, Texas: U.S. Youth Soccer, 2002.

Kaehler, Kathy. *Teenage Fitness: Get Fit, Look Good, and Feel Great!* New York: HarperResource, 2001.

Luxbacher, Joe. *Soccer Practice Games: 125 Games for Technique, Training, and Tactics.* Champaign, Illinois: Human Kinetics, 2003.

Murray, Bill. *The World's Game: A History Of Soccer.* Chicago: University of Illinois Press, 1998.

THE AUTHOR

Pete Farrow has a lifelong love of "the beautiful game" and has played and watched soccer for as long as he can remember. He has reported on soccer for British television, and for a variety of newspapers, magazines, and web sites in England. In his spare time Pete coaches a youth team, watches the game whenever he can, and is currently researching the historical involvement of money in soccer.

THE CONSULTANTS

Susan Saliba, Ph.D., is a senior associate athletic trainer and a clinical instructor at the University of Virginia in Charlottesville, Virginia. A certified athletic trainer and licensed physical therapist, Dr. Saliba provides sports medicine care, including prevention, treatment, and rehabilitation for the varsity athletes at the University. Dr. Saliba holds dual appointments as an Assistant Professor in the Curry School of Education and the Department of Orthopaedic Surgery. She is a member of the National Athletic Trainers' Association's Educational Executive Committee and its Clinical Education Committee.

Eric Small, M.D., a Harvard-trained sports medicine physician, is a nationally recognized expert in the field of sports injuries, nutritional supplements, and weight management programs. He is author of *Kids & Sports* (2002) and is Assistant Clinical Professor of Pediatrics, Orthopedics, and Rehabilitation Medicine at Mount Sinai School of Medicine in New York. He is also Director of the Sports Medicine Center for Young Athletes at Blythedale Children's Hospital in Valhalla, New York. Dr. Small has served on the American Academy of Pediatrics Committee on Sports Medicine for the past six years, where he develops national policy regarding children's medical issues and sports.

Index

Page numbers in *italics* refer to photographs and illustrations.

ankles 15, 38, *44*, 45
Argentina *8*, 12, 17

ball 40
    control 23–4, 26
Basten, Marco Van 15
Best, George 14, 17
Brazil 13, *16*, 17, 19, *33*

career development 56, 58–9
Carew, John *22*
cautions 14, 25
championships 12–13, 14, 15, 55
    see also World Cup
clothing *36*, 38–41
coaches 55, 56
colleges 58–9
commitment 20
competitions *see* championships
concentration 27
confidence 21
Cruyff, Johann 19

diet 31–3

England 9–10, 14
    leagues 20, 56
equipment 37–41
European Cup 14, 15, 19
exercises
    range of motion 34–5
    warm-up 33–5

*Fédération Internationale de Football
    Association* (FIFA) 10
flexibility *26*, 28–9, *30*, 34–5
fluid intake 31–3
foot injuries 43–5
Football Association (FA) 9
footwear 37–8, 39, 41
fouls 11, 25
fractures 44, 45, 53
free kicks 11, 25
Friedel, Brad *21*, 56

gloves *36*, 41

goalkeepers 11, *26*, *36*, 41
governing bodies 9, 10, 55, 56, 59
groin injuries 50
Gullit, Ruud 15

Hamm, Mia *54*, 55
Harkes, John 56
head injuries *52*, 53
heading 22, 24, 26
Holland 15, 17, 19

injuries
    contusions 48
    fractures 44, 45, 53
    knee 15, 17, *18*, 46–7, *51*
    overuse 48
    P.R.I.C.E treatment 43, 45, 46–7,
        48–9, 50–1, 53
    sprains 45, 47, 53
    strains 49–50, 51
    tendons 44, 45

Keegan, Kevin 19
knees 15, 17, *18*, 46–7, *51*

leg injuries 46–50

maintenance, equipment 39, *40*
Major League Soccer (MLS) 55
Manchester United 14
Maradona, Diego *8*, 17, 19
massage, 45, 46, 48, 49
Matthews, Stanley 14
McBride, Brian 56, 57
medical treatment *42*, 43, 45–8, 50, 53
mental preparation 20–1, 27
Milbrett, Tiffeny 20, 55, 58
muscles
    flexibility 28–9, *30*, 34–5
    injuries 45–51

Olympic Games 12
organizations *see* governing bodies
overuse injuries 48

padding 38–9, 41
pain 44, 45, 46, 47, 48, 49
Pelé 13–14
penalties 11
physical preparation 22–5, 27–9

physical therapy 45, 46, 47, 49, 51
playing surface 37–8, 40
preparation
    mental 20–1, 27
    physical 22–5, 27–9
    see also training
Protection, Rest, Ice, Compression, and
    Elevation (P.R.I.C.E.) treatment 43,
    45, 46–7, 48–9, 50–1, 53
protective equipment 38–9, 41

range of motion exercises 34–5
referees 9, 14
Reyna, Claudio *18*, 56
Ronaldo *16*, 17
rules 11

scholarships 58–9
shins 38–9, 41, 46
shoes 37–8, 39, 41
soccer, origins of 9–10
stretching *30*, 34–5
surgery 15, 45, 47, 48, 50, 53

tackling 25
thigh injuries 48–50
training
    action plans 20–1, 23
    speed 28–9
    stamina 28
    see also preparation

U.S. Major League Soccer 55
U.S. National Team 12, *18*, *54*, 55,
    57, 58
U.S. Soccer Federation 10, 59
U.S. Youth Soccer Association 56
ultrasound 45, 47, 48, 49

visualization 20–1, 28

warming up 33–5
women's soccer 12, 20, 29, *54*, 55, 58
World Cup 12, 55
    1958–1974 13, 19
    1986–1994 *8*, 17, *33*
    1998 *16*, 17
    2002 13, 17, 20, 55

Zola, Gianfranco 20